MENTAL HEALTH ENTREPRENEUR
A Guide for Entrepreneurs and Small Business Owners

Published by Therapeutic Play Foundation
Altadena, CA

Copyright 2018 Fields Family Counseling Services, Inc., DBA The Feel Well
www.ffcounseling.com
Printed in the United States of America

Names: Fields, Nakeya T., author. Kenner, Lisa, foreword. Barton, Kara, contributor. Reed, Leticia, contributor.
Title: Mental Health Entrepreneur
Description: First edition | California: Therapeutic Play Foundation, 2018
ISBN 9781948568005 (paperback)
Library of Congress Control Number: 2018903703
Subjects: Business, Health, Mental Health, and Entrepreneurship
First Edition: April 2018

Supporting a Charitable Cause:
100% of this book's proceeds will benefit the Therapeutic Play Foundation, a charitable organization 501 (C) 3 non-profit charity, whose mission is to build a healthier, more resilient world through empowerment, education and play. The Therapeutic Play Foundation in turn processes 100% of that amount towards costs of staffing, supplies, program development and research of play-based interventions for those who would benefit. To learn more about the mission of Therapeutic Play Foundation, or to donate to a worthy cause, visit
www.therapeuticplayfoundation.org

Therapeutic Play Foundation supports copyright. Copyright fuels creativity and promotes free speech. Thank you for buying an authorized edition of this book and for complying with copyright laws by not reproducing, scanning, or distributing any part of it in any form without permission. No part of this publication may be reproduced, stored in a retrieval system or transmitted in any form by any means, electronic or mechanical, photocopying, recording, scanning or otherwise except as permitted under section 107 or 108 of the 1976 United States Copyright Act, without the prior written permission of the Publisher.

Limit of Liability/Disclaimer of Warranty
While the author has used their best efforts in preparing this document, they make no representation or warranties with respect to the accuracy or completeness of the contents and specifically disclaim any implied warranties. The advice and strategies contained herein may not be suitable for your situation. It is recommended you consult with a professional where appropriate. The author shall not be liable for any loss of profit or any other commercial damages, including but not limited to special, incidental, consequential or other damages. The author did not create and does not claim to own any of the music or lyrics referenced.

DEDICATION

This book is dedicated to Amare, Richie Rich and Latte.
The fuel to my fire.

To my fellow social workers, this book is dedicated to all of you for your hard work, late nights, giant hearts and dedication to your clients. You are noticed and appreciated.

As for your aspirations, dreams and hopes…
may they manifest.

ACKNOWLEDGMENTS

My heartfelt thanks goes out to the people who held me up or reached out a hand whenever there were moments when I was sinking. A kind word of encouragement or words of support were so amazingly appreciated and propelled me through. Without you (my family, my friends, and my extended social media support system), I couldn't have felt supported and stable enough to take risks and believe in myself the way I've needed to on this journey.

My road to becoming an entrepreneur and author could not have been possible without all my family and I thank each and every one of you. I heart you much for listening to me with all my nonsensical passions and ideas and not being discouraging even when you didn't understand. Especially my mom, Lisa Kenner; my rock, my Bestie with a capital B and my most effective sounding board. My dad, Wayne Fields, AKA Albert, I acknowledge you for inspiring the hustler and crazy in me by birthright. My Nana, Nora Birks, who has always told me that the hard times "shall pass". That was the formative message that has served me best in laying the groundwork for a mindful life. And to the rest of the Fields Gang, so happy to come from a family with steel at its core.

To Richie Rich, I thank you because you are the best partner a Bonnie could ever hope for. I couldn't wish for a kinder, more supportive King. This actual book would not be a reality without you having my back. You got me and I got you. Amare, my handsome man: thank you for motivating me to be a better person to you and the world. Your birth and your status as a little Black boy full of joy has empowered me to strive for more because you deserve it.

To my colleagues and friends that have supported me and my efforts along the way with a conversation, a referral, a resource, a hug, or a learning opportunity…Thank you. Especially to my book contributors, Kara Barton and Leticia Reed. Thank you for your support and all your knowledge. The field is so blessed by you both.

To Beverly Lindo and Sylvia Gribbell… thank you for the dream walks and ventilating/therapeutic phone calls. They were worth more to me than you know. To Bill Hammond and Monique Smith, thank you for challenging me and teaching me what entrepreneurship and drive looks and feels like. To my Facebook family, if you've brainstormed an idea, threw me a resource, or shared your thoughts with me, thank you.

To Yoga, I am so happy that I found you as a practice. I have appreciated the calm and focus you have given me and how you have positively influenced my clinical practice.

To all those who have educated me, answered my invasive questions or directed me to the next step. Thank you.

To my artistic muses: Beyoncé, Christina Aguilera, Rihanna, Meghan Trainor, Janelle Monae, Big Sean, Bob Marley, Imagine Dragons, NF, Oprah Winfrey, and The Black Panther movie/soundtrack.

Thank you for the inspiration, power and affirmations.

"The attitude of gratitude is the highest yoga."
-Yogi Bhajan

FOREWORD

It was an early Friday morning in mid-October, when a young 17-year old girl started feeling what she thought were contractions. She felt concerned because her due date was still two-months away and it was too early to deliver. She was so scared. For so many reasons. Ten hours of labor and an earthquake later (yes, the world did shake while her baby girl was being born,) and despite every effort to stop the premature birth, a three-pound baby girl came into this world fighting for her life.

As that scared teenager, a girl with a tilted womb that had caused her doctor to advise that she may not be able to have children, I remember staring down at my sudden, unexpected… human that was my responsibility. I, who was both happy and absolutely terrified when I found out that I could, in fact, have kids and that I would have one and it was here and here a lil' too soon while still being a baby myself. I think watching my child having to stay in that hospital with needles in her head, reports that she may not live and weeks before I could hold her in my arms, prepared me to mother a fighter and to be a fighter myself.

Personally, I also think that my child being born during an earthquake and quite literally defying the odds by being conceived, was some sort of sign. Ever since this baby's beginnings, nothing has been able to shake or stop her from becoming the woman she is today. From the moment that I laid eyes on my bundle of joy, I knew that she was someone who was meant to be on this earth to make a difference. Her big personality showed right away that she was someone who cared about people and always wanted to help anyone that needed help.

Today, she is still my baby and I am so proud to see that she has flourished into this amazing, caring, smart, strong, brilliant and driven woman that can inspire others to be free and believe in themselves and their dreams. That woman is Nakeya T. Fields and I'm so honored to be able to provide the foreword on her book to introduce her to you as I see her.

Please utilize and gain from this guide for entrepreneurs and small business owners that my fighter of a "baby" worked to create for you…our fellow fighters. This book aims to empower thought leaders toward freedom from the grind. It includes real life stories of CEOs and strategies for monetizing expertise in the mental health field. There is also a digital download of Nakeya's 26 week Manifest It! Action Planner; an accountability tool to assist in manifesting and demanding the life you deserve.

Now, go get it.

-Lisa A. Kenner

Proud Mother of the "Mental Health Entrepreneur"

Table of Contents

Who Am I And Why Should You Trust Me?	13
Endorsements and Accolades	17
Queen Rising	20
My WHY	21
What I Want, Wants Me	31
Are You About That Life?	39
Stay Ready So You Don't Have to Get Ready	53
Resources	73
Say YES	80
'Cuz A Winner Don't Quit on Themselves	88
I Break Chains All By Myself – Won't Let My Freedom Rot in Hell	94
Summary and Action Steps	99
Build Your Business, Live Happier and Have More Freedom!	102
About Nakeya T. Fields	104
Book Nakeya T. Fields to Speak	107
One Last, Last Thing...	108

Who Am I And Why Should You Trust Me?

For the most part, the number one thing about my experience is that I've been in business and able to stay in business for more than a decade in this field. The whole time I've worked on my own and provided jobs for other therapists during that time. If you're interested in creating multiple streams of revenue in this field… I can help. I've proven that.

Others in this field are limited with their perspective. So many of us are trapped in private practice, living client by client, working a lot of hours. My intention is to show you that you can build a business by working your private practice, offering workshops and hiring others to help deliver quality services.

Let's talk about some of the factors that could stop someone from being successful in business… maybe they are a single parent… maybe they are a woman and have to fight social paradigms… maybe they're Black and have to deal with all that comes with that glorious state of being. Maybe they're unable to get funding based on how they look on paper – Black, female, single parent… so they're only approved for predatory lending. How do I know? I've been there.

I've always had to generate my money, every step of the way. I've sacrificed my savings, my retirement, my spare time, my time with loved ones… it takes a certain mental fortitude. That's what this book is about – it's not easy in business, and even harder with those factors present, so if you're not ready to take that on, it's that much harder.

Even more, if you don't believe that you will succeed, you're doomed before you begin. And it's disrespectful when others judge you for your success. I've had other therapists visit my office just to see what it looks like and then question how I got such a nice space. It's amazing.

Just to keep it real, this book is for business development. It's intended to help you grow your business as quickly and easily as possible by giving you fresh ideas about what you can do with your skills and expertise when packaged slightly differently.

This book was not intended to be a #1 Bestseller (even though that's what happened). It's designed to start a narrative conversation with you about your own potential, develop some trust and, ultimately, help you decide if we will work together someday.

While this book is short, it is packed with content you can use in very practical terms. My goal in sharing this information with you is to help you expand your professional horizons, live a better quality of life (if that's what you want) and set yourself up for long-term, sustainable success in business.

You're going to notice that I share some potential ways we can work together if / when it resonates with you. That's because my ulterior motive is that I want to help you reach and help more people, make more money and live with more freedom every day. At the same time, my intention is that you get value simply from reading this book. Either way, I'm honored to be in your world now.

Having said that, if you like what you read, *or most of what you read*, I'd absolutely, positively love to hear from you! Please share your success story or video with me at hello@nakeyatfields.com.

More than anything, please know that it's my deep-heart pleasure to help you treat mental illness while escaping the 9 – 5 grind and living an abundant life.

With good energy ~
Nakeya T. Fields

P.S.: I wrote and edited this book myself so you may find a spelling or grammatical error in it. If you do, will you do me a favor and tell me what you find by sending me an email to hello@nakeyatfields.com? Just note the page number, sentence and mistake and I'll fix it right away and send you a gift for your help. It was more important that I get this book in your hands than focus on perfection. (By the way, that's a secret for success in building a business!)

P.P.S.: If you love this book or make money through your business because of it, will you please post a review on Amazon? (And, if you DON'T like it, please send me an email, tell me why and I'll give you your money back, ok?)

Thanks again for your support. Here's to your success!

Endorsements and Accolades

"As the Vice President of Programs and Services for Aviva Family and Children's Services, I understand the importance of building and maintaining relationships. Fields Family Counseling Services has worked hard to establish trust, respect and connection within the mental health industry and has acted as a great community resource providing counseling and case management services directly in a practice setting. They also act as a temp staffing service that hires and manages mental health related positions for larger agencies. Their unique approach to satisfying an individual client's need as well as a larger agency's goal is appreciated."
~ Jeffrey L. Jamerson, MA, V.P. of Programs & Services, Aviva Family and Children's Services, avivacenter.org

"One of Nakeya's unique talents is to see what our future needs are going to be. She has always looked ahead and prepared our school in the best possible way. She can successfully work with a variety of personalities. She often goes above and beyond the defined scope to ensure that her clients get the best possible care and outcome. She works closely and effectively with the parents of our students for a more comprehensive approach.

Nakeya is able to connect to our student population in a way that establishes trust and confidence with the students. This is not an easy task. They look to her for guidance because they can trust her. She provides a consistent and connected approach that the students come to depend on.

Nakeya is an excellent communicator, collaborator and visionary. She has high standards and ethics and is, thus, very trustworthy."
~ Monique Baca-Geary, MA, Director of Education, Five Acres Therapeutic School, 5acres.org

"I have known Nakeya Fields for several years. I met when I was starting my private practice. I took her Social Worker as the Entrepreneur workshop and continued to network with her. She has been a mentor to me on all things business related in the field. Her mentorship has led me to grow my private practice, expand to a small business and continue to broaden my perspective of what I am capable of doing in this field. We do not get to learn the ins and outs of business in our social work program, however, Nakeya teaches you that and more! I continue to admire her work and all that she is doing to help those in our profession."
~ Ariel Macon-Richard, LCSW

"Fields Family Counseling offers an array of mental health services for children, individuals, families and couples. Nakeya and her team of therapists are trained and knowledgeable in various treatment modalities, including art therapy, trauma focused movement therapy, CBT and other individualized modalities to encourage self-growth in a safe and comfortable space."
~ Alyson Gould, LMFT, Los Angeles, CA

"Nakeya Fields brings radiance, sensitivity, and compassion to her work. She is a go-getter and a nurturer. Her expertise and experience in social work, counseling, and various kinds of therapy make her highly sought after when it comes to improving not only one's mental health, but their overall wellness as well. She embraces yoga, art, movement, music, and creative expression as modalities for healing which make her business, The Feel Well Empowerment Center, a holistic space that

provides her clients with the necessary support they need to thrive."
~ Bianca Cueva, Certified Yoga Instructor, Los Angeles, CA

"You want someone that is, caring, empathetic, honest, straight forward and just real? Then take a moment and have a conversation with Nakeya. She is equally comfortable with talking about the easy as well as the issues others may shy away from. Nakeya keeps her hands on the pulse and needs of the community and truly is a fighter of social injustice. Overall her Entrepreneurial spirit sums Nakeya up best. Someone who once you meet, your life will be enhanced for the better."
~ Kristle Manuel-Williams, ACSW

"Nakeya Fields has been a coach and mentor through my internship as a social worker. Her years of experience, compassionate heart, sharp mind, passion for the profession, and ambition bring tremendous value to the working relationship we have developed. I have found that her thoughtful approach to any situations that I encounter in my career was extremely helpful. I appreciate her for guiding me through starting my career, and for giving me the opportunity to intern for her."
~ Tanya Loussinian

"Ms. Fields brings passion and intelligence to all she does. In this book, she lets us share the wisdom and knowledge she has cultivated from taking risks to shape her creative professional journey, passing the baton to us, challenging us to have the courage to do the same."
~ Kara Barton, LCSW, RYT-200

"I am a social work intern and I find Nakeya to be an inspiration in the social work field. She is highly determined and driven. I look forward to working with her in the future."
~ Jessica Chapeton, MSW Intern

Queen Rising

If you are a therapist reading this book - which is written to be both a guidebook and an account of my personal story, I want to give you this moment of pause to imagine yourself as both a professional practitioner of the healing craft of mental health care AND the big boss. There is absolutely no reason why you can't be both. If you didn't think so before, it is my sincerest hope that this book encourages you to notice that you have choices and become empowered to take care of yourself, make change and manifest the career you desire.

I have written this book as a foundational support for those who are ready to make the leap into entrepreneurship in the field of mental health. My story is here for you for inspiration, education and best wishes toward your success.

~~~~~

As for me, when it comes to the work I do, I spend most of my time alternately engaging in therapeutic interventions with a small caseload that I pick and choose for myself or I'm networking, grinding and building the organizations that I have raised from infancy. Not only am I fulfilling a need in myself to utilize my clinical skills and help others; I do it on my own terms and on my own schedule in a way that fulfills me.

For me, that is living like a Queen. It is my opinion that we are always in control of ourselves since we are the Queens and Kings of our own vessels. That includes being in charge of where we take our bodies every day as well as what we do with it, our brain-power and our energy when we get there. If where you spend the most of your time (considering the average person working 40 hours per week for a standard 9-5 job) makes you miserable, it is your most important job as King or Queen of your vessel to protect your King/Queen-dom from the damage that misery (aka, stress) causes by being aware of it and making change.

My WHY

I don't quite know when I decided to embrace my quirkiness. I've always been a bit off to others. I could feel it. I could see in the pauses after Id said something no one else believed; an individual opinion that I quickly learned to stubbornly put out into the universe without needing a responding echo.

This started early for me because I've always been a reader. I remember having a large vocabulary from my early love of books and just wanting to live in my stories. I was a friendly, outgoing child, but I lived in a world of fantasy and books and big dreams from my stories.

In addition, I also had a cultural difference from many of my family and friends in that I was bi-racial. A frequent taunt was that I danced, talked, walked and had a butt like the other white people in my family on my father's side. I don't think it was meant to be cruel - I was different and people joked to deflect their discomfort at something being out of the norm or curious.

The people who assisted in helping me see my "other" in myself could see and understand that I physically looked different and well spoke about things they had no interest in. They could see I was interested in the topics I chose because I was (am!) a passionate little bugger. I was a bit aggressive in sharing and seeing if there were others just as interested in my interests.

Along the way, I attracted some people who wanted to observe my "crazy" and I pushed some away who thought I was annoying. I used to have a saying… you either hate me or you love me. Now my saying is: I love me. And that is all that matters.

But back then, I felt like an outlier and started to reference myself as "weird" as a point of identification to new people, because I could see my 'otherness' like a flashing neon sign – it was blinding. I wasn't quite sure if I liked it then. I think I just wanted to be the first to say it and warn them somehow… like a nonverbal announcement of "Beware, some of the words that are coming out of my mouth you may think are strange… roll with it!"

By the time I was an adolescent, my responses to basic questions were not age-appropriate and tended to edge on the fantastical or just too raw. I'd learned from books, so it made sense that I didn't quite know how to pronounce a word or that the kids I was around had no idea what language I was speaking. I always had some plan in motion, some dream of what I was going to attain.

And why not? That's what the characters in my stories did. The main characters always persevered, despite the hurdles they faced. The story usually involved a hurdle of a bad boy to conquer, a personal challenge, a recovery and a success - no matter how small - to follow.

My propensity to think like these heroes and heroines, and the corresponding personality that was forming, was most likely assisted by a steady diet of Harlequin romance novels about high-powered women who stood up to men and still deserved love. It was the cheapest books my mom could afford because I went through a book a day and, as a result, I was forming a mind interested in travel and love and possibility. Through my books I went to Australia, London, Africa… the best stories, the most exotic places, the most amazing people. And I wanted to experience it all.

When I reminisce now about my life experiences and how I got to a point where I knew entrepreneurship was for me, it is that recollection of feeling like the "other" that fueled me. And that feeling was not born of just looking different or feeling like I was just a bit awkward.

I was born premature and, according to some of my family, it was that early birth that made me "smart". That's what my dad says, anyway. I think he believes the fact that I went to college and work and keep an income is what made me smart. He also has some belief that preemie babies get bigger brains. I have no research to support that and believe that my brain is probably normal size.

Hopefully. But it tickled me to hear that I was smart with a big brain.

My mom put me in children beauty pageants, so I got the message that I must be pretty. I got to be in a "beauty" pageant at age one and I won a giant trophy as tall as me. My Nana says that on the day I was born, there was an earthquake and that meant I was supposed to be here to make an impact on the world. It was cemented.

So the deck of life is stacked in my favor. Not only was I smart and attractive, but now I can cause earthquakes and am special. I got all these messages of being special in fantastical ways during the developing years of my life. They served to instill an appreciated sense of confidence that was often tested by life and, to be honest, I have been tested most in my life by this journey into entrepreneurship more than any other experience.

~~~~~

When someone hears they are special, believes it and maintains the belief that they are special enough that - no matter what others think or say - they can attain the dreams that they want, the sky is the limit. We need to believe we can make the impossible happen when we are making our way through to becoming an entrepreneur, mental health or otherwise. We need to believe that some parts of life may literally suck the energy from us but, because we know we can do it, we will be able to make it through to the goal we have set.

Entrepreneurship is all about taking chances and having some of the chances we took come to fruition in the most exciting of ways, while others may crash and burn with feverish intensity. Being able to survive that rollercoaster of emotions takes a certain skill set and a stable support system.

It also requires you to embrace your own "other" status. Because if you are an entrepreneur in a world where we are taught to go to college, get a job, get married, have children and die, then… you are an "other" too.

Entrepreneurs live in the moment and risk and chance and many people see us as brave and amazing, like we are out there battling dragons. Sure, getting things up and running financially seems to equate dragon slaying, but if we all worked for ourselves, the resources would be more readily available and less 'every man for himself'. I'd hope, anyway.

~~~~~

In summary, my WHY is that I started embracing my sense of "other" at an early age and I realized in adulthood that every job I was in felt stifling and a bad fit. Like I was running around wearing a skirt that was too short and exposing my butt cheeks.

When I started to work for myself as a side hustle, I reveled in the freedom of choice. Eventually I was forced (in a way) by the universe to start working for myself in a full-time capacity. I became addicted to the choice of schedule and choice of clientele. I could choose which office I wanted to work in and if I had to work late or over the weekend. When I didn't make the correct choice, my bank account and stress levels paid for it and, thus, an education was attained.

I started to make different choices because I had to, when I had to, to make a living and a life for myself. Because I didn't have co-workers, I spent years in this cycle - a sort of never-ending tunnel of productivity and rest with an end goal of stability.

For a while, I existed alone. There were not many other mental health professionals in my circle who were fully self-employed and, if they were, it was in private practice. There wasn't a business model that was like mine so, again, when I spoke with my colleagues, I still felt like the "other".

I tried to share with my loved ones about the space I was in and they mostly just wondered when I was going to give up this crazy 'working for myself' thing. I only interacted with other therapists for about five years in employer/employee transactions. I provided them with part-time subcontracting opportunities via my contracts with various organizations. I often spoke to them about their own entrepreneurial endeavors, but most didn't want to move past the side hustle phase. And I was reminded of being that kid who felt like no one could understand my language.

Then I decided to further my education by taking more training in the business world because I had gotten to a place where I exhausted all my own knowledge and resources. I started to network with business owners outside the mental health industry. And it was there that I found my people. Off the wall people everywhere taking risks! They listened to my big ideas and thought I could do it! They'd done something similar, just in a different field and they'd talk with me about it all night if I'd asked. I was in outlier heaven. I've been there ever since and it's my land, man. The water is warm, the colors are vivid and the sunsets are sweet.

I'm working harder than I ever have now that I've found my people, because my people - these "others" - have supported me by being themselves in front of me.
By showing me that I'm not alone in this entrepreneurial world, I have been freed to continue to take chances, knowing that others have come before me and I can learn from them to make my own path.

But, as a mental health professional, I had a special bit of sauce. In business meetings where I'm pitching for a new contract, I can understand social cues. I understand how to build rapport. I understand the value of likability, active listening, reframing and problem-solving. And I can utilize my skills with absolute intent because they are part of me and I want to win and be successful.

I do not ever go into a meeting thinking I am not the best person to win their business. If you think anything other than that you are the best person for that business, the competition has already won. It is important for a mental health professional to be confident and utilize the skill sets they've learned in this profession. They need to apply those skills to winning the best clients for themselves and developing programs that clients will buy and continue to support.

Once you are there, in that place of confidence and intent, and are offered an opportunity, the idea of working for a paltry $20-$30 an hour will seem ridiculous to you. That is likely the moment you will realize that your income potential as a healer in a world that is hurting is unlimited.

If you don't do this type of work for money (which is weird, because why else would you work?), then I challenge you to also start a nonprofit and offer low costs or free programming in addition to the services you offer wherein you are compensated your worth. Generous people generate.

My WHY for becoming an entrepreneur was to find a sense of belonging within my status of "other". What's yours?

What I Want, Wants Me

The universe is not conspiring for you to fail – it wants you to be happy and successful. Since we live in an abundant universe, if you are not abundant right now, there is some lesson or opportunity waiting for you to claim it. Because if you want something bad enough, you can manifest it. What you want is seeking you right now.

Believe that. Know that. Live from that space.

If things don't work out for you, it just means it wasn't for you – it was for someone else. Your clients, contracts and opportunities are waiting for you. You just have to be ready.

Now, if you're not ready for those things, they may come in to your space but since you cannot do anything with them (due to being unprepared), they will keep going right past you. That doesn't mean they won't come back BUT think of it like a river – you cannot step into the same river twice. They will be different the next time.

We have to take action and energetic steps toward what we want… for example, to become a mental health professional, you had to take action by getting a focused education. You needed to apply for the program, then show up to the classes, then take the tests, then graduate. Throughout that time, you practiced lining your energy up with your end goal.

In other words, you have to want it, identify someone else who has it, learn from them, read about how to have it, then make the moves other success people have made until you learn how to make your own moves.

Also, when others know you want something, they will help you get it. That's how energy comes together – when you open your mouth and ask, and act on what you want, the universe can deliver on it in right timing.

That may not always be when you think, by the way. Timing might be something larger than you can see. For example, my mother was not quite ready to have me (as you read in the foreword) but it was my time to arrive – and that changed everything for both of us. There was a bigger plan than either of us knew.

~~~~~

In my own career, I went to Cal State - San Bernardino for my undergraduate studies for two years. It was natural for me to go there since I had good grades and was a cheerleader; when they offered a pilot program for all students with a certain grade point, I was automatically accepted. Otherwise, I would not ever have known about college at all because I didn't even have to apply - the pilot program's acceptance letter just arrived in the mail and I hadn't really made a plan to do anything otherwise after high school at that point.

While at Cal State, I met a friend who wanted to go to the University of Southern California (USC) and was sharing her interest in transferring. I didn't know that you could transfer mid-year to another school and it sounded like an adventure, and I was all about that, so I applied along with her, thinking we'd head off to Los Angeles together.

Ironically, my friend didn't even finish her application, but I did and I got in. There, I fell in love with the Trojan family and studied mass communications and popular culture at the Annenberg School for Communication.

My first job out of that undergrad program was as an intern with a special events company owned by a fellow entrepreneur, Bill Hammond. My first few months of searching for work after my undergrad program was frustrating. I wasn't sure what to do with a degree in communication. I ended up taking the aforementioned part time internship with Hammond Entertainment, where essentially, there were three of us interning for the summer. I wanted to learn marketing and how to run special events; my plan was to gain experience so that I can figure out my career path.

That summer, Bill, the owner, made an offer. One of his full-time staff was leaving - he needed to replace her and we all had the opportunity to have that full-time job based on performance at the end of the summer. It was like the *Hunger Games* and *Survival of the Fittest* combined. And kind of fun.

In the end, I won the job. That meant I had the opportunity to write proposals to gain business with large companies (like, BET, NBA All-Stars and Essence Magazine), learn how to sell, staff the events and handle whatever challenges came with each event. There was also a lot of travel involved and seeing how business operates from behind the scenes. That job was awesome and showed me the glamour of entrepreneurship and the inner workings of small business.

One day I'd just boarded a plane for a company trip, heading to the implementation of another successful event.

Suddenly it was announced that there was an emergency and we wouldn't be taking off as there had been a terrorist attack and planes were the target. They didn't let us leave the tarmac and, eventually, pulled us off the plane. That was when I learned that planes had driven into the Twin Towers. Fate was clearly on my side. We went home that day - the event cancelled.

Months later, the company had to lay me off because that event, 9/11 happened and they couldn't sustain having me as staff with the drop-off in business. They continued to use me on a contract basis to assist in writing their proposals. I agreed and did that for a while and random jobs as placeholders to pay the bills. I was using that time to think about what I could do for employment that would fit who I am as a person. The special events industry had been fun, and I'd learned a lot, but it wasn't quite for me.

Then I remembered in high school when I had no clue about where I was going next; and there was nobody to talk to me in a real way about my future and my options. I was a first-generation college student so I couldn't ask any family how they applied for college or financial aid themselves. I decided in that moment to be a counselor to help kids know their options for their future.

After some research into my options I chose to pursue a graduate degree in social work as my tool to find employment in a down economy. I had developed a plan to attain a Masters of Social Work in order to qualify for a position that was not related to special events. That's how I discovered the industry of mental health.

My last year at USC, I worked with the County of Riverside for my intern field placement. My family had suffered a loss – my cousin had passed away – so I needed to be close to home but still drive to Los Angeles (LA) twice a week. For a year, I did that drive and, when I did, I agreed to help other social workers with their site visits. It was a hardship to do that drive. It wasn't easy to find the time to do those site visits.

Eventually, when I graduated, those same social workers got promoted to be leaders in the county and asked me to contract as an adoption home study writer, to assist with their overflow of clients. I suddenly had a side hustle with a nice income that I came to depend on. One day, that side hustle reached out to let me know that they had changed the way they assign subcontracted services. An individual like myself no longer qualified to work in that capacity on a 1099 basis as a sole proprietor; instead, that work needed to go to a business via a contract. So... *"Would I be willing to become a business and bid for the opportunity to keep providing that service?"* they asked. I decided to go for it. I said, **Yes!**

I had no idea how to do that so I went to the library, I approached my former teachers who knew more about that stuff and I studied. I went to the city office and asked questions. I created my business structure using google and books as a resource and figured out how to write an RFP (Request for Proposal) by using an old copy of a grant proposal I'd written for a school project. Part of my strategy was to rope my school friends into doing home studies with me and offering all of us as service providers for the RFP so we had group power in getting the work done – and it worked. I won the contract!

The moral of this story is that the crisis in my family helped position me for that opportunity. A hardship of driving to LA was an opportunity to help colleagues out; give some relief from a heavy caseload. They returned the favor by believing in me to provide quality services and they thought of me when an opportunity came around that they thought I might fit. I couldn't possibly have known how things were going to turn out. This all took about 10 years to play out.

The bottom line: karma is real. And relationships matter.

~~~~~

What you want wants you… when you think about what you want, make sure to go beyond what you think is possible to what you really want. Because when you tune into that, you magnetize it into reality. You manifest what you really want at your deepest, most feeling level.

Are You About That Life?

Before you take the tenuous steps toward working fully for yourself, an important question to reflect on is:

Am I about that life?

The life of the entrepreneur, mental health or otherwise, is one that requires a slight comfort with risk, bravery and resilience. It requires innovative thinking as you build your own path.

When I first started my private practice, I had no idea what was going on and I had to learn through trial and tribulation. My education to become a Master of Social Work (MSW), unfortunately, did not come with a handy guide with knowledge and resources to avoid every financial and personnel related pitfall of business building. Combining resources from online google searches, library visits and interviewing other business owners, I taught myself how to build my business when I was given opportunities.

I learned how to recognize a potential opportunity for my business when reading articles or listening to others at business networking events. I then researched how I could be involved with said opportunities immediately or I wrote it down or texted it to myself to look further later. Research led to action, then more action and, eventually, I started to understand how to make the foundation of my business more stable.

As I was going through that process, I was contacted by many of my colleagues in the field asking how I was doing it because they noticed that I hadn't yet gone back to a full-time job and I seemed to be happy. Meaning, I seemed not quite so miserable, as was the industry norm when you are overworked in environments that create the need for you to find time to reboot after sharing so much of your energy with and for others.

How was I working fully for myself using my mental health license? Maybe I had some secret guideline to share that would make a successful business happen for them so they too could escape late night paperwork, insane hours and mental exhaustion of meeting billable hours, etc.

In thinking of how I can provide some reference on how to describe a successful path in entrepreneurship, my mind turned to all the amazing people who had been a part of *The Social Worker as an Entrepreneur* workshops that I held each summer.

Many of the people who participated were just licensed or had been licensed for a bit and weren't quite sure how to begin the process of establishing their business and being competitive for clients. Some were not yet licensed but had entrepreneurial opportunities that they were excited about nourishing.

Either way, they shared a commonality of wanting more for themselves and needing a starting point and a community to make the leap. The workshop I held was geared toward providing a lot of info about the initial steps in starting a business and the resources to do so, as well as some step-by-step instructions on how to get paneled with insurance companies and win contracts to provide services directly instead of through a middleman (an employer).

Following the workshop, all participants became members of a Social Worker as an Entrepreneur mentee listserv group that served to offer continuous encouragement to build business. Amazingly, we still communicate to this day and share resources. Shout out to the SWAE group!

Because I've seen many in the SWAE group go on to have successful and thriving private practices, become highly sought-after as authors or speakers, or they've been able to procure direct contracts as service providers – all entrepreneurial endeavors, I thought that incorporating a few of their stories of their path toward mental health entrepreneurship would be beneficial.

Exposure to real life success stories of those willing to brave the hills and valleys of business planning and growth is something that is worth its weight in gold, for it shows that if they did it, you can do it too.

Kara and Leticia were both in the 3rd cycle of the SWAE workshop and continue to be some of the most active members in utilizing the listserv to support others and to share their successful endeavors.

Kara was working in the Neurology department for a major University feeling a bit entrapped by the full-time status of her job. She was in the workshop to figure out a way to explore working for herself in some capacity while keeping her position because she liked it. But she wanted more time for herself and more freedom to be creative with her knowledge and skill set.

Leticia was in a similar space - she'd already started a private practice and had various side hustles while working full-time at a large mental health agency. She had gotten a few contracts as a freelance provider but wanted to scale her efforts up a bit to not have to work so much and burn herself out with too many jobs.

Both SWAE participants started with a small part-time private practice on the side of their full-time job to determine if that way of business was for them. That has since morphed into an exciting status as experts in their particular niche. Now, they both travel the country educating and completing seminars in their realm of expertise. This transition was possible because both made efforts to take action toward getting more education about how to fulfill their goal. They joined a community to learn how to build and maintain a business, networked with like minds and had a plan.

I now introduce you to Kara and Leticia, Mental Health Entrepreneurs who have escaped the traditional 9-5 grind and successfully monetized their expertise.

In their own words…
Mental Health Entrepreneur: Kara Barton, LCSW
Kara Barton, LLC – Los Angeles, CA

I like to know the rules. Then I can break them or work within their confines, as needed. I trusted Nakeya, having met her in graduate school, and then having watched her blossom into a strong, creative entrepreneur. She had done the heavy lifting of finding her way through the requirements and regulations of early business development, and I wanted to bask in her light and glean from her knowledge.

Most of the attendees to the SWAE training were younger, aspiring, energetic people, like Nakeya, ready to take on the world and build their empires. I was not. I was a middle-aged woman, still energetic with a full-time job, but looking for ways to move through the world with more freedom, fewer restrictions, and conceptualizing how to dip my toes into the world of private practice with an eye on long term sustainability into future retirement.

Using the resources and ideas I obtained in the SWAE training, I started a small private practice after reducing my full-time job to 80%. I located space that was reasonably rented by the hour and began promoting myself via word of mouth.

Due to my niche (neurological conditions/caregiver issues/chronic illness), I had access to organizations and thus was able to tap into alternative revenue streams. I had a gentle flow of referrals and found my way into a comfortable light caseload. It turns out that what I really needed was to know I could do it. And, I actually really needed to decrease my workload and increase my self-care. I have been able to oscillate between rest and work using this alternative day to vary my schedule.

I am now in the process of creating new projects that include training, travel and telehealth. I can see how these projects and ideas will bloom into a model that will be sustainable into the future. Creating this extra space to explore ideas and move into areas of work in which I was not sure I would fit has been exciting and liberating.

Although at the SWAE follow-up meetings I was an outlier, it has been gratifying and inspiring to see other professionals take off with their own unique ideas. We each have the fundamentals to create our own visions, to offer our skills to the world and, at the same time, keep our own self-care in the equation.

Mental Health Entrepreneur: Leticia R. Reed, MSW, LCSW
Reed Behavioral Solutions – Manhattan Beach, CA

I received my license (LCSW) in January of 2012 and opened my solo practice immediately. My decision to venture into the unpredictable, yet rewarding, world of entrepreneurship after working multiple years in the public sector was driven by my personal desire to provide compassionate, authentic and individualized treatment to others, specifically underserved populations.

My approach was to tailor my business to address the varying needs of individuals that the fast-paced, productivity standard-driven, high case load and "one size fits all" public mental health sector made it difficult to provide. I obtained my LCSW in the state of Nevada while still maintaining licensure in California and transitioned my solo practice to one that now offers a variety of services beyond the four walls of the office setting.

Because of this transition, I've been afforded the opportunity to provide direct services to individuals while assisting behavioral health agencies establish effective mental health infrastructures to expand quality mental health service delivery and normalize mental health treatment to make significant strides that will ultimately eradicate the negative stigma attached, specifically for people of color where cultural factors contribute to fears and prevent many from seeking treatment.

I've been blessed to be able to diversify my passion, talents and skills into multiple streams of income by adding services such as: in-person and video conferencing trainings, workshops, public speaking both domestic and abroad, individual clinical supervision for Masters of Social Work and Marriage and Family Therapy interns seeking licensure as well as Association of Social Work Board Examination (ASWB) coaching for Master of Social Work interns preparing for the National ASWB exam to obtain licensure.

In addition to these services, I continue to serve on professional panels, appear in professional articles and maintain a social media presence to continue to raise global awareness of mental health issues. I want to educate new mental health entrepreneurs on how to demonstrate integrity, compassion and authenticity while creating a thriving and lucrative business in the mental health field without losing themselves in the process.

My achievements were accompanied with plenty of growing pains, all of which have sharpened my business acumen. Being an entrepreneur and, in my case, a "solopreneur" is a very tedious, arduous and yet rewarding journey. From marketing and other overhead costs to constantly assessing the changing trends and balancing the appropriate amount of exposure and remaining competitive while not diluting the ethics and integrity of the field, one can become quite overwhelmed.

As a novice entrepreneur, I often overextended myself and believed I needed to accept every opportunity offered to gain exposure but gradually learned how to hone my craft via professional trainings and mentorship. Additional certifications and degrees to increase my skills sets and marketability also followed my now "work smarter and not harder" philosophy.

My increased marketability, due to my additional trainings, has allowed me to be more selective in choosing the platforms and partnerships that would benefit me as opposed to ones that depleted me and ended in adverse business relationships. I've also learned that the passion and reason for entering the field must always remain the primary focus as this keeps one afloat throughout the highs and lows that are inevitable for any entrepreneur, specifically for those in sole proprietorship.

Most importantly as a mental health entrepreneur, I've learned my professional worth and continue to illustrate this in my business negotiations. People tend to undervalue our work and assume that "healers" are supposed to do the work of helping others for the sheer love of it, without adequate compensation. Having a solid understanding of your worth is extremely important and can make the difference between an enjoyably satisfying, profitable career, versus one that is filled with dissatisfaction, burnout and financial lack.

During my journey as an entrepreneur, I've formulated a list (5 R's) of practical "ingredients" that have conjointly proven successful, allowing me to live my BEST life with passion and purpose which I would encourage others to follow.

1. Be Authentic and REAL

Stay true to yourself and never compromise your authenticity and uniqueness.

2. RUN Your Own Race

Stay in your lane, focus on your personal path and life course and move at your own pace.

3. Be RELATABLE

Remain approachable and willing to constantly evolve and learn in spaces outside of your comfort zone and with individuals who are different from you.

4. RETREAT Often

Unplug and PAUSE from work periodically to refresh and to develop new ideas and creativity.

5. REAP Your Harvest

Enjoy the fruits of your labor and do not feel guilty basking in your accomplishments. Life should not be all about work.

~~~~~

I think it's obvious why I'm so committed to this work. And I want to help you enjoy the same kind of results through your own mental health business.

Manifest It! Action Planner

A 26-week Accountability Tool

Get your Digital Copy NOW at
www.NakeyaTFields.com

The Manifest It! Action Planner was initially developed as a therapeutic accountability tool for me to use with clients I was coaching toward a goal.

By putting words to paper, you set intention and that works to manifest your goals through action and planning.

This Planner encourages that action items be identified, responsibilities be assigned and deadlines honored. It is specific and motivational because it also reminds about self-care.

You need action to manifest your goals but you also need the time and rest to pause to be able to think clearly and make sound decisions.

When you think, plan and care for your physical vessel and spirit, you will feel better and have more to offer others.

Writing helps to ingest the good - it is your first action step toward attaining your goal. Use it as a tool to revisit and be reminded of your intention to succeed.

Thank you for reading my book and please utilize this action planner to assist you further in making moves to Gain Freedom and Escape the 9-5 Grind.

Get your Digital Copy NOW at
www.NakeyaTFields.com

Stay Ready So You Don't Have to Get Ready

Mental Health professional careers often follow a common trajectory. The professional attains a Bachelor or Masters degree to build a career. If they have a Bachelors degree or less, the most common types of positions available are case management and/or safety and risk assessment or maintenance programs like wrap-around, parenting programs, child protective services, etc.

Those types of positions don't require intensive clinical expertise and, because of that, the income opportunity at this level seems to be limited. This is also the "social worker" that is depicted a lot in movies as the beleaguered figure transporting a just-abused or soon-to-be further traumatized child to a new placement or new resource. This figure is an obvious necessity to move the story along and isn't usually depicted in the best light and they don't seem as if they are happy folk raking in the change. Think *White Oleander*, *Lilo and Stitch*, and *Precious*.

A Masters level therapist can often be found in some of the case management, non-clinical positions as well, but they do have the option of attaining licensure and, thus, expanding their income streams in ways that Bachelor's level-professionals cannot attempt to procure.

There are title protection issues with regard to the title "Social Worker" because those with a Masters-level degree in Social Work are called social workers just as the case management social workers with any required education are called social workers. Those who do the work to attain a Masters degree often don't appreciate the comparison and there has been many arguments for why those working in case management and are not yet masters level or licensed should not be able to have the title of social worker. It is these types of arguments that started Masters-level social workers and the industry to call themselves Clinical Social Workers.

Those who go to graduate school to attain a Masters in a clinical field, like Social Work or Marriage and Family Therapy, upon receiving their diploma attain their clinical experience in a position straight out of graduate school. This is often for low or no pay because agencies are aware that these persons need the experience and hours for their career enhancement. Some of these positions are more case management or crisis interventions/resource provision while some are clinical.

Many Masters-level professionals work at agencies offering counseling services and receive clinical supervision so that they can utilize their experience and hours to become licensed. Once they are licensed, they can open their own businesses providing counseling services to the public without a go-between. They can also open practices before they are licensed, if they have an agreement with a clinical supervisor to review and sign off on the work. More on that in a bit.

Most often, getting licensed means the Clinical professional gets a raise at their current job. That fact motivates a lot of the professionals to pursue the license in the first place. This is because the agency that employs them can now bill a higher rate because they are licensed. If the mental health professional chooses to start their own business or private practice once licensed, they can receive 100% of client's payment/fees instead of just getting a cut from the employer. Just a thought. Notice that thought.

Another common trend amongst licensed mental health professionals is to offer workshops, clinical supervision to unlicensed professionals, retreats and trainings. They also often engage in speaking engagements or become an author to establish expertise in the field for increased exposure and clientele to be able to charge higher rates. This is the level of social worker that engages in research and becomes an author to share that data with the world and also build programs around the data and/or use it to gain funding and exposure for further research. We often see this level of professional in the movies as a couch shrink or busy doctor figure like in *Donnie Darko* or the television show *In Treatment*.

Whether Bachelors or Masters or Licensed, all professionals can start and establish a thriving business. A Bachelor or Masters-level professional just has to get creative and hire someone with a license to sign off and supervise, if that is a necessary requirement for their income stream. Often it is not - there are opportunities out there for all levels of mental health entrepreneur if only they are willing to let go of some of their resistant thoughts and find them. The number one resistant thought I've heard many mental health entrepreneurs speak when they are consulting to start a business and leave their full-time job… "I can't leave, I wouldn't have health insurance and I need that". That thought keeps them at their position for another ten years or so until they get "the insurance" for life or something like that.

I have mentored and hired some of the most talented clinical therapists and many have faltered in going after their own dreams because they don't want to lose their jobs' health benefits or a severance or some other promise your job made to keep you in forever servitude. I challenge this thought with how much easier it would be to pay for your own health insurance or save more of your income after you have had such a large increase in income from getting 100% of your cut when seeing clientele (or at least more than 50% if you join a group practice and allocate some of your income to helping that group practice run). It might be hard to have the discipline to allocate monies for those expenses once you get your full cut of your income, but it would save you money in the longer run when you are able to do so.

Speaking of income, we in mental health are not known for being numbers people. We often find trouble when it comes to finances, especially when the professional has a side hustle in addition to their full-time job and are paid as 1099 staff/subcontractors. That 1099 status does not require the mental health entrepreneur to pay taxes on the monies they make. Thus, it requires them to save up money to be able to pay out for their tax responsibility when the time comes. It can be a shock come tax time that the income made from their side hustle can result in a large personal tax bill and all the taxes are due immediately on what can be a large number if you've had the side hustle and paying no taxes on that income for the full year.

Most times, if a mental health entrepreneur is working in that part-time capacity, they are operating their brand as a sole proprietorship and that sole proprietorship is usually linked to their social security number. Business entities with their own employer identification numbers (EINs) separate from a personal social security number of the owner; will be able to attain more funding opportunities and will be in a better position organizationally.

A sole proprietorship, according to the State of California Franchise Tax Board (FTB) website, is the simplest and most common form of starting a new business and consists of only one individual and has no existence apart from its owner. A couple can be considered an "individual" as well for the purposes of a sole proprietorship, but more than one unmarried individuals is considered a Partnership. All rights and responsibilities are in the hands of the individual.

The FTB describes a general partnership as two or more persons who agree to create a business and share the profits and losses. All persons involved share equal rights and responsibilities in managing the business as well as full personal liability for the debts and obligations of the partnership.

An LLC, Limited Liability Company, is described by FTB as is a hybrid business entity that blends elements of partnership and corporate structures. Businesses that provide professional services requiring a state professional license, such as legal or medical may not form an LLC.

When I was forming my first business in the field, I applied for an LLC and was denied because it was a professional service (i.e., medical - if you can bill health insurance). I learned this first hand and that's why I chose to become incorporated as an S corporation that provides the same protections but is not limited by mental health being a professional service.

An S corporation generally offers liability protection to its owners (shareholders) and is a conduit where the profits or losses of the S corporation flow through to the shareholders, partners, or members. An S corporation does not pay federal income tax. Under California law, the S corporation is subject to a 1.5 percent tax on its net income and is a conduit similar to a partnership. Each shareholder is responsible for paying taxes on their pro rata share of the S corporation's items of income, deductions, and credits. S corporations are subject to the annual $800 minimum franchise tax (State of California FTB, 2018).

Mental health entrepreneurs would benefit from being aware of these type of issues as they established themselves as a business. As a clinical social worker, **my advice is not that of lawyer or accountant** and if you want to confirm for yourself, I'd recommend a consult with a professional.

Personally, I have had the benefit of over 10 years of working for myself both in private practice and as a Director of multiple programs and multiple contracts. I am the founder and chair of a nonprofit, and a Director of a corporation with multiple DBAs, income streams. With that in mind, I share the process by which I have been able to create and maintain those business entities in a way that allows me to maintain a positive relationship with money and the tax system.

My route was sole proprietor for two years and then I became incorporated as an S-Corp once I knew I made enough income to save the $800 per year minimum required for the tax responsibility. I also needed that incorporated status to win some of the larger contracts once I began to scale up the business to grow larger, serve more clients and make more money.

The S-Corp status allowed me to claim expenses of the business (all costs I incurred to keep the business running), and then what was left over in the income statement after claiming the expenses is what rolled over to be claimed as "personal income' for my personal income taxes. I'd recommend you keep receipts or keep a business checking account opened with your business' EIN (which you will learn more about in this chapter) and make all purchases you intend to claim from there. I'd recommend linking that bank account with a Quickbooks program or a Quickbooks Online account, or one similar (runs about $40 per month expense) so that come tax time, you'd just need to send a report to your accountant to show him/her all the expenses. Or maybe you already have a bookkeeper reconciling and keeping track of that for you, or you can handle that on your own. That's up to you and your accountant or bookkeeper. It is definitely recommended that you consult with someone in that profession when you start making a steady flow of income through your business.

Items to consider if you are just starting out:
- Who are you and how would you like to be seen?

- How would you like to expand your brand?

- How can you use your current network to create opportunities?

- Are you ready to make the leap to being fully self-employed now or do you plan for a slow roll out of a part time practice while you maintain your employment?

Responsibilities as a Business Owner:
- Appropriate licensure/supervision of service providers. Protect yourself and your business by hiring providers who meet the requirements according to the Board that governs your state's mental health providers.

- *Taxonomy Code*: This is the type of mental health professional you are. There are several options including Clinical Social Worker, Behavioral Health, etc.

- *Business License* (city where your business will operate): Get one of these by going to your local City Hall, Chamber of Commerce, etc.

- *Business/Malpractice Insurance* (HPSO, CPH & Associates, NASW related): Malpractice insurance is usually necessary to sublease an office or to win a contract with an organization.

- *CAQH* (Council for Affordable Quality Health Care): This is a resource for those wanting to be on insurance panels on private practice. Usually have to be invited through an insurance company but you can contact them directly to explore options. https://proview.caqh.org

- *EIN*: Must obtain an Employer Identification Number (EIN) to have your business monies tracked differently from your personal money. It is free of charge and can get it usually within 48 hours via the IRS website. You can apply for one EIN and have multiple businesses operating under alternate names called DBAs or Doing Business As.

For example, my business - Fields Family Counseling Services - was the company name I applied for initially with my EIN but I have an additional business that utilizes the same EIN to receive monies under another name, The Feel Well. That was done as a branding decision to separate out a new service offering.

To learn more about EINs, please visit:

https://www.irs.gov/businesses/small-businesses-self-employed/employer-id-numbers

- *NPI* (Individual vs. Organization): An NPI is a unique identifier developed by Centers for Medicare and Medicaid Services. The allocation of these identifiers is governed by the National Plan and Provider Enumeration System (NPPES).

According to the Centers for Medicare and Medicaid Services website, a mental health professional must apply for a NPI number because of the Accountability Act of 1996 (HIPPA), mandated increased security in communication for health care providers and health plans. You can apply as an individual or a business.

If applying as an individual, you own this NPI and can assign multiple locations. Your job does not own your NPI, even if they are the ones who helped you apply for it. When you leave that job, you can go to the NPPES website and remove that location of your old job as well as add the location of the new one or the location of your new business.

When applying for an NPI as a Organization, this means that other individuals can list their NPIs as assigned to your location and then, if you own a group practice, you can bill for their NPIs. You do not have to be fully licensed to attain an NPI. You can be registered with the Board of Behavioral Sciences as an intern but remember, as an intern, you need a fully licensed supervisor to sign off on any services. For more information about the NPI, visit the NPPES website.

https://nppes.cms.hhs.gov/NPPES/Welcome.do

Communication and Accessibility:
- **Can your clients find you and contact you?**

- *Phone/Fax/Voicemail system*: RingCentral, Grasshopper, One Talk, etc. These are VOIP/Internet based phone systems that transfer your business number to your cell phone. You can answer and run your business from wherever you are. Most of these services come with an auto-receptionist and is a great resource. You can have a 1-800 number and if you have a staff, you can offer extensions to your main number as well.

- Website presence: This is necessary in a digital world. If you do not have a website for your business, you are behind. People cannot find you, share you or just sign up for working with you on the go. People are on the go nowadays and their phones are always in the hand. It is your best and easiest way to interact with prospective clients. Your web site is always up even when you are sleeping. That means your website could be your conduit to potentially making you money while you sleep. Read that again. You, a mental health professional, can make money while you sleep. You can sleep and have a life and make money too. Whoah.

- *Intake Packet*: An intake form is useful to onboard new clients. It usually includes confidentiality clauses, policies enforced, etc. We utilize Intake Q for our current electronic Intake system. We like it. It is a way for prospective clients to be able to go to our website and directly submit a HIPPA compliant and detailed intake report as well as their insurance information all on their own. Your business would just have to create your intake in a Word document, upload it into Intake Q's online platform and they will convert it to an electronic form that can be embedded into your website.

All my business has to do once a client submits their intake packet online is review the intakes, verify benefits if they are using insurance, and schedule the intake appointment. The completed intakes are downloadable and we file them electronically in our practice management system - also web-based. This process assists in taking away a lot of the headache of onboarding. There is a cost, so this is a service that might be a part of the scale up of the business once you have enough to cover the monthly costs of these types of services (generally $20-$30 per month).

-*Practice Management System*: My practice has gone through several web-based Electronic Health Records, practice management systems. I won't endorse any but I will name the options I know of such as Therapy Note, Therapy Appointment, KASA EMR, Simple Practice, Theranest, TherapyMate, Therasoft, Psyquel, etc.

I do recommend that a electronic, HIPPA-compliant practice management system is used. You can use paper intakes and locked file cabinets to keep files secure initially, but really most things have become electronic and it might be easier to start with a practice management system so you don't have to transition. Of course, that is up to you, entrepreneur.

Investment:
- **Where are you in your ability to invest in your business (Finances and Time)?**
The saying goes… "You have to spend money to make money". I agree. You have to create a foundational system that will make you money, but it will cost to set that up

initially. Are you ready for that? Let's explore ways you can make money and how you could set that up.

- Private Practice Model/Billing Insurance and/or Private Pay

If you are setting up a private practice, you can charge per session a set rate. Cleary outline your fees and policies regarding your practice in your intake packet. This is harder to make bigger amounts of money because people prefer to use their insurance for therapy costs or often don't have the funds to sustain recommended treatment. However, there are many private pay only practices out there.

For insurance billing practices, you must be able to set your business up to bill effectively because from what I can tell in my experience, insurance companies don't like to pay mental health professionals for their time. They pay mental health CPT codes much less than they'd pay a medical CPT code from an MD and they give us the absolute most frustrating, throw the phone at the wall run-around when we try to call them to understand why they are trying not to pay us for the time we worked with the clients they referred us.

This frustrating trend has caused all sorts of billing services to pop up as businesses because they see we poor mental health professionals were losing money and becoming victim to what seemed to be predatory panels that seek ways to not pay us when they know we've seen their clients and provided services. A billing service basically provides persons to call the insurance companies on your behalf if there is a billing issue and hound them until you are paid. It's like your own collections service.

This billing service can be buried in the costs of your practice management system and they bill on your behalf once you've had a session and watch when there are errors for you. I recommend a billing service if you are planning to bill insurance. It might save you some of the headaches I've encountered.

- *CMS 1500* : The standard form to manually bill funding sources for mental health services. Available for sale at office supply stores or usually completed through a billing clearinghouse, like OfficeAlly, electronically.

- *Create a Panel Letter* to mail out to insurance companies expressing your interest in joining their panel. You can also hire a company to get you credentialed with the insurance companies you are interested in. I have found this to be a worthy investment as dealing with insurance companies can be time consuming with wait times on the phone.

Purchasing/Contracts:
If you win a contract with a large organization to provide a service or for your business to provide a service, that can act as an ongoing referral source. A guaranteed income via a contract referral source; clients mean income. Income means stability.

- Have you considered becoming a Minority Business Enterprise (MBE)?
To be an MBE means that your business is certified as being owned by U.S. citizens and is at least 51% minority-owned operated and controlled. (A minority group member is an individual who is at least 25% Asian, Black, Hispanic or Native American.) When this is the case, you can qualify to get funding opportunities that MUST be assigned in each state. For example, most states have to meet a certain percentage of business with MBE's and most are not even close. There is a lot of recruitment for MBEs but the certification can be rigorous, which daunts entrepreneurs from even trying to be certified. That's a potential opportunity for you.
http://www.mwbe-enterprises.com/mbe/

- What about becoming a Women Business Enterprise (WBE)?

Also, a similar type of opportunity exists for women as a WBE. http://www.wbenc.org/

- What about qualifying as a Small Business Enterprise (SBE)?

Similar unique opportunities exist for small businesses - http://www.dgs.ca.gov/pd/Programs/OSDS/SBEligibilityBenefits.aspx.

- *What is the benefit of contracting/becoming a vendor?*

As a business entity, you can register on procurement sites as a vendor to be able to provide services. Different agencies have procurement sites, like the City of Los Angeles or County of Riverside. They each have their own procurement or purchasing department to manage and recruit their service providers.

If you are interested in providing direct services to a specific organization, it might be beneficial to search for their purchasing or procurement page. If they have one, register your business as a vendor. That status as a vendor will entitle you to invitations to the email you signed up with to submit bids or Request for Proposals (RFPs).

Those Bids usually invite you to submit your qualifications and your best plan to provide services on their behalf. You cannot be a sole proprietor and register as a vendor and win bids. The RFPs usually outline the requirements of eligible business entities. If you do not yet meet the requirements of an opportunity you are interested in, it might be useful to use it as a guide to build your business' structure so that you can be ready to apply for it in the next cycle of funding.

What exactly is a Bid/RFP?

Investopedia.com indicates that a request for proposal (RFP) is a type of bidding solicitation in which a company or organization announces that funding is available for a particular project or program and invites companies that have registered as vendors to can place bids to have the opportunity to assist with the project's completion. This is the way to have a company/organization as a regular referral source of clients for your mental health business. It takes away you having to rely on making money individual client by individual client; instead start thinking bigger about making money individual contract by individual contract.

It's important to choose organizations that you enjoy, support and feel match your ethical outlook. Ensure that they service the clients in the way you prefer. Do your research. If you do not take this in mind, you will just end up with another job you hate, but this time you have to pay all the expenses and handle all the administrative worry.

Networking is important as well when you are submitting bids. The organization's purchasing/procurement departments are made up of real people - people who are probably in the field. Get out there and network and see what opportunities are out there for you to bid on! Register as a vendor and stay current about new opportunities to win bids.

Remember - business growth only happens when you take action. This book is accompanied by a 26-week action planner and accountability tool that can assist in this effort. Take advantage if any of this spoke to you. You can download it at nakeyatfields.com or get the spiral bound version at www.theMHEbook.com.

Resources

Because I am a Cali gal, my resources are based in California. However, you can use these as a reference for what to look for in other states in the U.S.

- BidSync: www.bidsync.com

- Planet Bids: www.planetbids.com

- Los Angeles Sheriff's Office:
http://www.lasdhq.org/lasd_contracts/info.html

- Los Angeles County: http://camisvr.co.la.ca.us/lacobids/

- Orange County:
http://www.ocgov.com/ocgov/Business/Bids/,%20Auctions%20&%20Purchasing

- Riverside County:
http://www/purchasing.co.riverside.ca.us/document/open

- Sacramento County: www.saccountybids.com

Networking/Marketing

Check Meetup.com for groups that you might want to connect into your community around special interests.

Networking is the magic ability. Hone those skills! For my tips, I make certain to get the person's name, title, email, mobile #, web address and company name at a minimum.

I also have found Instagram and Facebook to be effective business networking tools. Most businesses now have a social media presence.

Therapist Databases:
A good opportunity to spread word of your new business venture is a database listing. When I first started my business and was signed up, they averaged 2 clients per week in referrals minimum.

Affordable and most also offer a resource of a journal and web-based community included in the investment.
- Psychology Today
- Goodtherapy.org
- Find-a-therapist.com
- Therapistlocator.net
- TherapyTribe.com
- Mytherapistmatch.com
- Therapy on the spot

Website:
www.NakeyaTFields.com
My practice is fully electronic. A client can submit an intake packet in the middle of the night and we will get in the morning and be able to follow-up. A web presence is very useful in today's digital business environment where smart

phones, IPADs and technological magic rule the day. It helps business flow, can keep data and provide reports. A website is the new business card and gives you credibility.

Social Media:
- Office Marketing
- Linkedin / Facebook / Twitter
- Understand image usage requirements
- Therapy sites
- Blogging (Blogger, Wordpress, etc.)

Colleague Support:
- Referral source
- Partners in Service provision
- Support system
- Collaboration to win larger contracts

Referral Sources:
- Mass mail campaign
- Contracts/Purchasing Agreements
- Physician referral
- Word of mouth
- Cold calling
- Niche programs
- Court Systems
- Niche websites

- Colleagues
- Schools
- Hospitals
- Book - Become an author expert to establish authority

As your brand grows, there are things to consider:
- Payroll
- Health Insurance
- Employees vs. Contractors
- Incorporation (an S Corp recommended for this industry, but consult with accountant about your specific situation)
- Office space – sublease hourly, as needed then multiple days per week, then full-time.

Recommended Reading:

• *The Business of Psychotherapy: Private Practice Administration for Therapist, Counselors, and Social Workers* by Robert L. Barker

• *Successful Proposal Strategies for Small Business: Using Knowledge Management to Win Government, Private-Sector, and International Contracts* by Robert S. Frey

• *Start Your Own Business* by Rieva Lesonsky and the staff of Entrepreneur Magazine

- *Bids, Tenders & Proposals: Winning Business Through Best Practice* by Harold Lewis

- *Small Business Resource Guide* offered by the IRS (Order a copy www.irs.gov or by calling (800) 829-3676)

- *Power or Presence: Unlock Your Potential to Influence and Engage Others* by Kristi Hedges

Inquiry Form

Nakeya T. Fields Inquiry Form

Fill out this form to stay in touch, schedule a meeting with Nakeya to discuss building your business as a mental health entrepreneur.

Your Name: _____

Business Name: _____

Mobile Phone: _____

Direct Email: _____

Website: _____

What do you want to discuss with Nakeya?
- ☐ Business Coaching with Nakeya as my mentor.
- ☐ I want to join one of Nakeya's programs.
- ☐ Have Nakeya speak at my next event.
- ☐ Promote Nakeya's programs and services as an Affiliate/JV Partner
- ☐ Other: _____

Please Attach Your Business Card to this Form
OR Text "Call Me" to (323) 422-4093
to Enter This Information Digitally

Say YES

In my practice, a common response I have to someone in the room who is seeking change is "what are you changing into?" This often stumps my client, so I'll rephrase.

Where would you like to be at the end of your journey to change? What does it look and feel like to you? Let's talk it out… What changes are you going to make in your life today to start yourself towards the path of manifesting that change?

I then ask for some homework to be completed on their own time where they write out what that plan could look like at the end.

For example, it could mean that, if you want to leave your depressing job, then the only alternative is to make yourself the best candidate for a position that doesn't make you depressed.

One way of manifesting your desires is that if someone offers you an opportunity that is directly in alignment with the path you've identified and you can see that if you went down that path it could lead you closer to your ultimate dream… you must say yes.

Say Yes. Say Yes to everything, learn from your mistakes, be tired, ask for help, but say yes… or you will stay right where you are. That first yes is the first of many. But when you give yourself the gift of saying yes and saying it often (even if you don't think it's what you want in that exact moment or it's a by-product of a bigger yes), it will teach you something. You will be stronger for it and further along the path toward your bigger goal.

There is no such thing as failure – only unexpected outcomes. Those scenarios are really the best way to learn because you have to apply what you know in a new way.

Besides, the people who don't 'fail' are the people not trying anything at all. These are the people who say no to something unexpected, unknown or unfamiliar simply because it's outside their comfort zone. Ironically, you must step outside that comfort zone in order to grow to your next best level.

I can prove that I have lived that journey…

I became fully immersed in entrepreneurship as a result of when I was a full-time social worker at a school. I got paid summers off. It was probably the best job you can get in our field and still have a job.

However, I had two clients who were Black males, ages 9 and 10. I was seeing them all year for mandated services. These kids started sharing that their special education teacher said they would never amount to anything and that their teacher would give them drugs to keep them manageable.

I tried to help the teacher, based on the school's leadership, to motivate the children. I observed her class and found reason to confront her about the drugs. Amazingly, she said the drugs wouldn't hurt them.

I tried to report her to Children's Protective Services (CPS) but they said it was up to the school to investigate. I went to get an advocate to fight for the children and, the next day when I arrived at work, I was blackballed and threatened to back down.

The teacher told the parents they couldn't get an advocate. That in itself is illegal. And it is what cemented my commitment to not work with that kind of a system. I was the bad guy for advocating for children.

At that particular school system, if you worked for them for less than three years, you always got a lay-off letter every June. They didn't want to pay salaries over the summer. Predictably, I got my letter that June. I'd gotten it last year too, and just like last year, a rescission of the lay-off notice came just in time for the new school year to start. I could go back to work if I wanted. This time I did not accept the offer and I said No. I was empowered to make change for my community – as a Black woman and a future mother. And so, I quit.

At the same time, I had my adoption home studies business on the side and decided that I was going to create my own economy. I looked for part-time contracts, like 10 hours a week, for licensed social workers, that would enable me time to build my business and provide income to cover my expenses. When I saw a school that was offering a 5-10 hour / week job for a licensed social worker, I went for it. That job was at a therapeutic, non-public school.

They wanted to pay me $30 / hour for 5 hours a week. I negotiated at least 10 hours / week so I could afford to live. I had already downgraded my living to a friend's basement so I could afford to grow my business with the home study services as well as my private practice and the 10 hour / week cushion from the part-time contract.

However, I negotiated a rate increase (so I could afford to live) AND I negotiated that it would be a contract as a business using the EIN number – vs. a job with my personal social security number on a 1099 – because I wanted to have other providers help support the contract.

~~~~

Note: it is vitally important that you consider having a business structure for the most responsible approach to taxes and asset protection. As a business, you have protection if someone decides to file a claim against you. You also have the benefit of filing taxes through that business. When you are working on a 1099 basis using your personal social security number, you are open to losing your home, your car and other property should any claims arise as well as being taxed all at once which can be financially debilitating.

~~~~

By the time my original school employer came back to give me my job in the fall, I said NO. I said it with a hope and a prayer. And that was my turning point.

Three years into the contract with that second school, I was up to running the whole program and hiring a staff to service it and we still hold that contract today. That contract led to other contracts with large organizations throughout Los Angeles. My private practice is thriving and has expanded to a wellness center. It's a significant achievement – and I know you can do it too.

The bottom-line: my contracts manifested because I said yes to a little part-time job, that I converted into a contract, because I had to escape a system that abused children and pretended it wasn't happening. I needed to be able to advocate for children with strength and power.

You have to be confident in your services to negotiate your value. That's how my business grew – the 10 hours / week contract plus my ability to create programs and add therapists to support those programs was one of my strategies.

Now, I have to share one other part of this adventure with you.

During that time, I was pregnant. I carried low and, as a result, had to be on bed rest for the last two months of the pregnancy. My then-partner was not supportive of my business. I had no income. And yet, I submitted a 'Hail Mary' proposal by saying I have a full staff who can provide services under my management and I'll provide personally when I get return to work.

And they said no.

The whole rest of my pregnancy, I worried they were going to replace me with another option. They could have hired someone else but, fortunately, it happened that I had created a value system when I was there through providing quality therapeutic work, as well as being a good businesswoman.

Money is not the only success factor – it's also about service provision and creating the relationships between yourself, the entrepreneur, and your client who hires you.

At any rate, during those two months, chaos ensued – my programs fell apart. However, when I came back, my proposal was accepted and implemented to provide counseling and speech services to the school. I came back with a full staff and triple income. As a result, I was able to manage the programs for the whole school.

The point I'm sharing here is that opportunities don't always look like you expect them to and, sometimes, you have to shape them to fit your goals. That takes clarity, fortitude and an ability to negotiate as well as pivoting to meet the circumstances and think two steps ahead.

So say yes, fail forward faster and celebrate all that you're learning as you go. Just say yes.

'Cuz A Winner Don't Quit on Themselves

Business has the power to take you out even before you begin because mental health practitioners don't typically think of themselves as entrepreneurs. Setting up the business structure, handling the paper, writing the grants, getting the insurance, handling the difficult patients, setting up a referral network… these are just some of what can take even experienced practitioners out of the game.

But a winner don't quit on themselves – that's what Beyoncé says. And I'm here to tell you that's the truth.

When I was a Children's Protective Services (CPS) social worker out of grad school, I was in a program that paid $20k for every year you worked for CPS. Why? Because it's such a hard job that they pay your college tuition to lock you into working it.

It was the most stressful, traumatic experience you can imagine. When I was an emergency response worker, I had to get to the scene even before the police. Because that means you are in dangerous situations, you need to work in pairs. People don't like it when you're questioning their parenting. Nobody liked seeing our white car pull up to their door.

Sometimes, in the emergency response role, you were still on call, even if you had already worked your full work day, because you were on duty and had to be ready to respond to an emergency until your duty time was over. Usually a 24-hour period. I felt an anxiety all the time to be prepared to handle an emergency. Then when I went to handle it, I was seeing children who had been abused by their own parents.

Sometimes I had to wrest children away from their parents. And sometimes I would go back two months later and see the same children being abused again in the same home. It's emotionally traumatizing to see that kind of abuse over and over every day. Hence, the reason for the pay that locked us in to CPS. We got a sort of prepaid hazard pay via graduate school funding.

One of the other tragedies of this situation is that my partner never showed up. She would just call off. It was so interesting for me. Later, I came to realize that we all have that other person who is supposed to help hold us accountable but they're just not there. And, you can't blame that person for not being there. In this scenario, I felt alone but I shouldn't have to depend on another person to do right by these children. It shouldn't be such a hard job that we need to work in pairs.

As a mental health professional, we're already giving of ourselves to help heal and support others and to do it in those types of environments is brutal. After about four years, I had to go out on stress leave – I had heart palpitations and I thought I was dying. My gums were bleeding, I was losing hair, and I was going to happy hour every day after work. I was gaining weight rapidly because I was drinking and not exercising and working so much to try to get the funds together to go on vacation to escape my life. I didn't have a love life because I was overworking and not giving my body the right nutrients so I didn't present as a happy and healthy person who was attractive inside or out.

It wasn't a healthy place in my life or my career and I remember my breaking point.

I went to do an investigation for domestic violence. There were babies. We had helped a mom escape the previous month, moved her to another house out of state – and there she was again, back in the same house. Everyone in the home was cognitively delayed so they didn't understand what was really happening. The father was abusive, especially when he was drinking, so we had to remove him. The family was hostile about our removing him or removing the children to keep them safe.

Making the decision to keep children safe by removing them from the home is not easy. I remember taking a child out and I called police for an escort per protocol. I had an intern with me. We followed the protocol.

We walked in with the police to remove the child and, for the first time in my experience, the police intervened and said they wouldn't let us remove the children. But I was the one who called them out for the escort to do that very thing. I didn't know how to react — I'd never had a police officer countermand my recommendation. I don't make decisions on my own — others had concurred, including my supervisor. So I let him know that this was our only option. He proceeded to call back-up and, when the other officers showed up, they surrounded me so I couldn't take the baby.

I had to walk through them with an intern following me, a toddler by the hand and a baby in the basket, with five officers following and yelling at me. Because of me doing my job, I felt threatened. I got us all into the car, drove off and immediately burst into tears. The intern was empathetic while I had to watch these children for five hours until they were placed back at our office, not really getting a chance to process an experience that had been traumatic for me. And then I had to do the report for court, get ready for the hearing, and not be appalled at what I had just been through in that situation.

At that moment, I could have dropped the field of social work. I could have walked away. I could have said I don't need to do this. But I feel I keep being exposed to these children being hurt, being hurt by the very systems that are supposed to protected them. And it inspires me to be an entrepreneur, to create real options for people, to create a new system that actually works.

Needless to say, I quit that job. I went out on stress leave. I saw a therapist and a psychologist who told me I had a propensity for alcoholism because of my coping skill of happy hour visits, that I was going to have a heart attack and, basically, told me to take three months off.

When those months were up, I wasn't ready to go back. After six months, I'd decided I couldn't go back for my own health. My home study business was my income and I started at an inpatient facility part-time to get the hours to get licensed, so I could have my own private practice one day. If I didn't do that, my business wouldn't be as lucrative in the field of mental health because, without a license, I wouldn't be able to bill independently for services. I was supposed to be medicated to go back to work but, instead, I used that time to think and plan how I could move myself and my business, which has become a extension of me at that point, forward.

There are multiple takeaways from this story; essentially, the mission of my business is about helping people and finding creative ways to do it. My strength is people, especially when I see their suffering and how some systems do not always provide the type of support that is helpful. My purpose is to work with other providers and my clients to deliver quality therapy and services to the people who need them. And no matter what I encounter along the way personally or professionally, I didn't – and I won't – ever quit.

The Queen is here.

I Break Chains All By Myself – Won't Let My Freedom Rot in Hell

Many people mistakenly believe that being a mental health professional means you should live hat in hand, that doing good means you have to sacrifice. I'm here to tell you – and SHOW you – that's just not true. You cannot be afraid to talk about money because that fear manifests as a repelling energy. Think of money as your friend so that it wants to come and hang out with you. Visit and go on vacations and brunches.

We live in a positive universe, where your natural talents and skills are your path to abundance. That path is easier when you are the one defining it by being an entrepreneur. What is easy for you is what you came in with to share with others because others have different gifts to contribute. So just because it's easy does not mean that it doesn't have value.

Go big or go home. There is no try - only do. To get big contracts, you have to think big. Feel the fear, know that's a sign you're in motion and do the big, scary thing anyway. Being in business requires a level of fearlessness that you might not believe you are capable of experiencing. In fact, you were made to be free. You are committed to helping others live a life of freedom. And so, you must breathe and experience your own freedom.

You must believe you can do it. You have to value the people you are going to help more than you honor your fear. Nothing gets to be bigger than you in your life or in your business.

And there is no half-assing it – you must choose to be an entrepreneur or an employee. In my opinion, it is too difficult to do both because you cannot be spreading your wings to soar in your own business and then clipping them to build someone else's dream as an employee. If you are still working a full-time job while you grow your business with the goal of eventually working only for yourself, you are an entrepreneur. If you work a full-time job and are counting the years until you retire, you are an employee.

Choice is the most powerful force on the planet – even more than love, because you have to choose to love. Sometimes love pushes you beyond the bounds of reason. And that kind of love is what will pull you beyond the bounds of your comfort zone… your love of self, the life you want, the abundance that is yours, the people who need and are waiting for your support and more.

So invest in your own self-care. Break the chains of your self-saboteurs. See the possibilities as they are rather than by what you think you can have… and work toward those. And build relationships – they are both the work and the way to gain new work.

Mental health professionals have a unique opportunity right now in that the world conversation is all about mental health. World leaders are taking us down some unexpected paths. Programs are closing, funds are drying up, children have unmet needs… you are the professional who has chosen to champion mental health. It is up to you to act to make a bigger difference through your education, training and expertise.

And, whether positive or not, all eyes are on the mentally ill. Who treats the mentally ill? Us. This is our collective challenge and our greatest opportunity.

We need to collaborate with each other. Our society is very individualistic – what's mine is mine. We tend to follow the private practice model, where we live client by client, or the group practice, which is the same in bulk. But there are larger opportunities that are currently being monopolized by the organizations that have staff to write the RFPs and the know-how and connections to win the opportunities over smaller options like you and me.

So, by being aware of RFPs and the opportunities available to us as mental health professionals, we could collaborate and take on those monopolies to deliver quality care. But we have to do it together. We must hear the calling and marshal our forces collectively to make it and create change.

Altogether, the net result of all of that I've shared with you here in this book is that I encourage you to become a mental health entrepreneur. By doing so, you can have greater influence in treating mental illness, gaining freedom, escaping the 9 -5 grind while monetizing your expertise.

"The act of putting pen to paper encourages pause for thought, this in turn makes us think more deeply about life, which helps us regain our equilibrium." ~ Norbet Platt

Note to Self: You have just finished a download of information. Release the most immediate take away thought here. Pause, notice it. Write it here to save it for later when you develop your first week's action plan. Free write, now – in this moment:

Summary and Action Steps

"Know Your Otherness"

My goal for you is to show you that, when you continuously invest in yourself to upgrade your experience and take care of yourself, you have more to share with others.

You and everybody you know has been through hard times and you're still standing. In fact, you know about human dynamics and human potential like few in this world do as a result of your education and training. But you are not here to suffer. We live in an abundant universe – it's time for you to know your power to create and manifest the life you want through your chosen profession.

I know this to be true because I've done it. Against the odds… a black single mother in mental health, building a business instead of taking a job… well, I broke the mold on how you're supposed to do this stuff. After serving hundreds of mental health professionals to inspire and support them in achieving the business and lifestyle of their dreams, all I can say is that I wish I myself knew 20 years ago what I just shared in this short book – it would have made my journey a lot easier.

It's not easy to create significant change – and yet, your future depends on it. The life you really want to live, and all the people you will help by feeling happier, healthier and more satisfied with your life, needs you to step up and out in a new way.

If all you did was create an extra $1,000 / month by having a business, would it be worth it to you? For many, just that much can be a real game-changer… and you can do a whole lot more than that by having your own business.

It all begins by making the choice – today – to become a mental health entrepreneur.

In closing, I encourage you to drop me a message at hello@nakeyatfields.com or visit my web site at www.NakeyaTFields.com to take advantage of tools and resources to help you build and grow your business to make a bigger difference in the world. If you are a fan of social media and want to join me as I motivate with tips on self-care and business; you can follow me on Instagram and Facebook @TheFeelWellCoach.

As I said in the beginning of this book, "Know Your Otherness" – it's what sets you apart as a unique individual and it's the secret to successful business.

In any case, please keep me posted on your progress!

-Nakeya

Build Your Business, Live Happier and Have More Freedom!

It's Possible! Join A
Business Accelerator Program

ASSISTED EMPOWERMENT PROGRAM

Individualized business and/or lifestyle for those seeking empowerment toward the goal of an improved lifestyle or fulfillment of business-related goal. Short-term and long-term options.

ESTABLISHING YOUR BRAND PROGRAM

This accelerator takes place over two days and is for the entrepreneur that has already established a business and is stuck and seeking the scale to the next level of their business. It is also ideal for a start-up business that needs guidance in ways to build a solid foundation for growth and stability. Participants are provided with the knowledge, tools, tips and resources to help develop the right strategy for you and your business as a brand in a 2-day workshop intensive.

PUTTING THE AUTHOR IN AUTHORITY PROGRAM

It's time to step out of that tiny box that the world has created for us, and step into our power using our insights, experience and know how to share what we know from a position of power and authority. Nothing does that for the academic and behavioral health professionals like being published. Join this program and jumpstart your new reality as a thought leader, influencer and authority in your field of expertise. We offer you step-by-step assistance as you take control and present yourself to the world as a Best-Selling Author. Act now! Your "Author"ity awaits!

About Nakeya T. Fields

Nakeya T. Fields, LCSW, PPSE, Registered Play Therapist-Supervisor, Trauma Informed Yoga Therapist (LCS 25754/RPT-S 1619)

She loves being a mom to her son, Amare. She also enjoys yoga, reading, being outdoors on a sunny day, singing out loud and trying new things.

Nakeya is an alumna of the University of Southern California where she received a BA in Communication, a Master's in Social Work and a Pupil Personnel Services Credential in School Social Work and Child Welfare & Attendance. Nakeya is also a Registered Play Therapist - Supervisor and a certified field instructor and clinical supervisor.

Nakeya is a 200 HR TT Yoga instructor, certified in trauma informed yoga therapy and is certified in Mini Yogis Yoga for Kids yoga. She is licensed by the Board of Behavioral Sciences as a Licensed Clinical Social Worker in the State of California.

Nakeya is the owner of Fields Family Counseling Services, Inc & The Feel Well Empowerment Center, which provides wellness resources such as counseling, therapeutic yoga, messy art classes, play therapy, socialization and support groups (www.ffcounseling.com). She is also President and Chair of the Board for the Therapeutic Play Foundation, a nonprofit that seeks to build a healthier, more resilient world through empowerment, education and play (www.therapeuticplayfoundation.org).

Titles by Nakeya T. Fields, LCSW

Black CEO: Black, Brilliant and Built for Success, 2018. Contributor.

Manifest It! Action Planner: An Accountability Tool For Those Ready To Wield The Power Of Their Will To Make Their Dreams Come True, 2018. Author.

~~~~~

Nakeya can be reached to book a speaking engagement, business coaching or to learn more about the Business Accelerator programs through the following venues.

Speaking, Coaching, and Book related inquiries: www.nakeyatfields.com

Telephone: (323) 422-4093

Fax: (866) 488-8170

Email: hello@nakeyatfields.com

Mailing Address: 530 S. Lake Avenue Suite 236
Pasadena, CA 91101

Affiliated Web Sites:

Fields Family Counseling Services, Inc.:
www.ffcounseling.com

Therapeutic Play Foundation:
www.therapeuticplayfoundation.org

The Feel Well Empowerment Center:
www.thefeelwell.com

Book Nakeya T. Fields to Speak

Book Nakeya T. Fields as your Keynote Speaker and You're Guaranteed to Inspire and Motivate Your Audience!

Nakeya is available for book signings, speaking engagements, seminars/workshops, coaching and consultation.

For more info and to book Nakeya for your next event, visit www.NakeyaTFields.com OR, call +1 (323) 422-4093.

One Last, Last Thing…

If you enjoyed this book or found it useful, I'd be very grateful if you'd post a short review on Amazon. Your support really does make a difference. I read all the reviews personally so I can get your feedback and make this book even better.

If you'd like to leave a review, then all you need to do is click the review link on this book's page on Amazon here:

www.theMHEbook.com

Thanks again for your support!

THE END

The light in me sees the light in you.

Now let's get out there, and let it shine.

www.ingramcontent.com/pod-product-compliance
Lightning Source LLC
Chambersburg PA
CBHW070031040426
42333CB00040B/1533